I am I
Therefore, I am Self
Therefore, I am All Things Yet No Thing
But most importantly
I am
— Ricco Pierre

Virtus unita Fortior.

Nil sine vobis

Per Nos omnia

Pulchritudine tuâ captus sum

Ulterius te vinciam

Regeneratio tua in

Per te vivam

W.F. fe:

101

Aphorisms

of

Alchemy:

Discovering The

Secret of Secrets

Baro Urbigerus

Ricco Pierre

HRMTC ALKMY
REVEALED IN PRACTICE

Title: 101 Aphorisms of Alchemy: Discovering the Secret of Secrets

Based on *Aphorismi Urbigerani*, originally published in 1609

Attributed to: Baro Urbigerus

Edited and Modernized by: Ricco Pierre

Publisher: HRMTC ALKMY Publishing

Published by:

HRMTC ALKMY Publishing, LLC

924 N Magnolia Ave

Ste 202 Unit 5073

Orlando, FL 32803

USA

ISBN: 979-8-9912723-0-8

Library of Congress Control Number: 2025939446

First Edition: 2025

Cover Design: Ricco Pierre

Printed in USA

For more information, visit **hrmtcalkmy.com**

Contents

Notes from the Editor

In editing this transcript, I aimed to render this *Work of Art* in a modern tongue while preserving the integrity and directness of its subject matter. First published in 1609, *Aphorismi Urbigerani, or Certain Rules Clearly Demonstrating the Three Infallible Ways of Preparing the Grand Elixir*, by *Baro Urbigerus,* remains a cornerstone in the Hermetic tradition.

I gently restructured several aphorisms to maintain a consistent tone, rhythm, and grammatical structure throughout the manuscript. These adjustments do not alter the original meaning; instead, they enhance readability for contemporary readers while retaining the cadence, emphasis, and conciseness intended by the author. I preserved all *Alchemical* nomenclature, which created emphasis within the author's literature.

Where historical phrasing introduced ambiguity or obscured meaning, I incorporated subtle clarifications to support comprehension, always strictly following the author's conceptual framework. At no point were interpretive liberties taken with the principles or symbolic structure of the text.

This *Work* serves as both a procedural guide for practitioners of the *Great Work* and a spiritual-philosophical treatise encoded in the operative language of Alchemy. Its balance of concise instruction and divine contemplation places it among the most unadulterated and purposeful writings of the early modern Alchemical practice. Including both the *Circulatum Majus* and *Circulatum Minus* significantly enriches the text, offering readers a dual initiation into the Mineral and Vegetable Kingdoms.

This edition was prepared with deep respect for the original source, clear responsibility to the modern reader, and a commitment to preserving the authentic voice of one who demonstrated personal mastery of the Art.

Introduction

TO OUR DEAR DISCIPLES, HONORED
COADEPTS, AND ALL WELL-WISHERS TO
OUR HERMETIC ART.

*F*inding you, dear Sons, who have—through our guidance—
attained the proper knowledge of our first Matter and are now
worthy to receive further Instruction in the remainder of the
process, we present this to eliminate any Ambiguities you may have
conceived during our Absence. We aim to facilitate your Labor and
provide precautionary advice to help you bring your Work to its highest
Perfection.

*According to your request, we now offer you—and, for your sakes, to
the Public—the most infallible rules necessary to avoid Errors in this
significant Undertaking. Although you, our ever-honored Coadepts, have
not yet come to a Resolution to present the World with the complete Practice of our Art joined with the Theory, we are confident you will not
reproach us for making these Rules public. We have written them so that
even those unfamiliar with our Person will immediately recognize the
absolute Truth in our words. They will see both the Theory and the Practice
of the Hermetic Art and conclude that these Operations have undoubtedly
passed through our own hands, as evidenced by the precision and infalli-
bility of the Instructions we provide—illuminating the most obscure
Enigmas of the Philosophers and warning of all possible Accidents in
working with our Subject.*

We are confident, therefore, that you will not, and indeed cannot, blame us for this. You will discern that our sole Design is to instruct our Disciples and protect this noblest Art's sincere Well-wishers from being deceived by any false or pretended Adept. Our goal is that all those who, by Divine Benignity and through the help of these Aphorisms or otherwise, have received the blessed knowledge of our first Matter—which is the same in all three of our methods for producing the grand Elixir—may through these specific Rules, accomplish their Desires.

During our travels, we encountered individuals with proper Principles in Philosophy and Religion. We embraced and instructed them in the further Perfection of this Celestial Art, through which—by comprehending the Mystery of Mysteries—we also learn to serve God in Faith and Truth. Furthermore, since we owe no living Soul for the knowledge we possess—having attained it solely by the Blessing of Almighty God upon our Industry and Expense—we consider ourselves at greater liberty than those who have received such Favor through us or another Adept. Therefore, we are determined to continue doing the same whenever we meet qualified people.

Being in England—though we are not Native to this Kingdom—we find it necessary to set forth these Aphorisms in the English Tongue. We trust that the discerning reader, focused on the Sense, will easily pardon any Impropriety in our Expressions. Furthermore, should Providence carry us into another Country, we, possessing a competent knowledge of most European Languages, shall endeavor to publish them again in the Language of that Place. In doing so, we hope to more swiftly accomplish our Desire: to undeceive the World by presenting certain and evident Marks that distinguish the Worthy from the Unworthy and to guide Men away from unnecessary Forms by instructing them in the proper way of Serving God—the only path to happiness in both this World and the next.

The Grand Elixir
CIRCULATUM MAJUS

I

Hermetic Science consists solely of acquiring correct knowledge of the *first Matter of the Philosophers*, located within the Mineral Kingdom and not yet determined by Nature.

II

Because an undetermined *Matter* constitutes the origin of all Metals and Minerals, those who comprehend and recognize it will readily understand their respective Natures, Qualities, and Properties.

III

Although some individuals—misguided by erroneous beliefs—imagine that the *first Matter* exists only in specific locations, seasons, or through the action of a Magical Magnet, we affirm with certainty, following our Divine Master *Hermes*, that such notions are false. The *first Matter* exists universally, is accessible at all times, and is discoverable only through our Science.

IV

Hermetic Art consists of the precise Manipulation of our undetermined Subject, which must undergo all designated Chemical Operations before attaining the highest degree of Perfection.

V

Our prescribed Chemical Operations include Amalgamation, Sublimation, Dissolution, Filtration, Cohobation, Distillation, Separation, Reverberation, Imbibition, and Digestion.

VI

When we refer to these Operations as ours, we do not equate them with the conventional methods of the Sophisters of Metals, whose efforts merely disguise the Subjects from their Form and Nature. In contrast, our Operations aim to truly transfigure the Subject while preserving its original Nature, Quality, and Property.

VII

After undergoing all the artificial Operations—each designed to imitate Nature—this Subject becomes the *Philosophers Stone*, or the *fifth Essence of Metals*, as it consists of the Essence of the four elemental Principles.

VIII

Metals and Minerals that have already been determined by Nature— even when reduced into running *Mercury*, Water, or Vapor—cannot be the *first Matter of the Philosophers*.

IX

Our authentic *Matter* is a Vapor impregnated with an undetermined Metallic Seed. Created by God Almighty and generated through the

Concurrence and Influence of the *Astrums*, it resides in the Bowels of the *Earth*, which serve as the Matrix of all created things.

X

We refer to this *Matter* as undetermined because it serves as a *Medium* between a Metal and a Mineral—belonging to neither—yet possesses the intrinsic power to produce both, depending on the Subject it engages.

XI

We refer to such a Metallic Vapor, congealed and nourished within the Bowels of the *Earth*, as the *undetermined*. When it enchants the *Serpent* with the allure of its internal and additional Fire, it becomes the *determined Green Dragon* of the Philosophers. No progress can be made in our Art without the actual knowledge and precise Manipulation of our *undetermined Matter*.

XII

The *Green Dragon* is the natural Gold of the Philosophers, fundamentally distinct from Vulgar Gold, which is corporeal and dead, having reached the end of its Perfection according to Nature. Vulgar Gold cannot generate unless first regenerated by our *Mercurial* Water. In contrast, our *Green Dragon* is spiritual and living, possessing the generative Faculty within itself and its own Nature, having received the Masculine Quality from the Creator of all things.

XIII

We call our Gold *Natural* because it cannot be produced through Art and remains known only to the true Disciples of *Hermes*, who understand how to extract it from its original Lump. For this reason, it is also called *Philosophical*. Had God not graciously created this first *Chaos* within our reach, all our Skill and Art in constructing the *Great Elixir* would prove in vain.

XIV

From this Gold—our *undetermined Green Dragon*—without the addition of any other created substance, we employ our *Universal Menstruum* to extract all the Elements or Principles necessary for performing the *Great Work*. This constitutes our first method of preparing the *Grand Elixir*. As this first *Chaos* incurs no cost beyond the labor of mining, we aptly name it the only way for the Poor.

XV

The Operations in this first method closely resemble those in our second, in which we join our *determined Dragon* with our *Serpent*. To avoid unnecessary repetition, we shall provide unified Instructions for both methods in the subsequent Aphorisms.

XVI

Our *Serpent*, also contained in the Bowels of the *Earth*, represents the closest Feminine Nature to our *Dragon* among all created things. Through their Copulation upon an astral and metallic Seed containing our Elements, this *Serpent* must likewise be brought forth. Though it requires more Expense and Time, it can perform the entire Mystery of *Hermes*.

XVII

Because our *Serpent* is the nearest Feminine counterpart to our *Dragon*, she must, after Copulation, serve as the Basis of our Philosophical Work. From her Bowels alone—without assistance from any other Metal or Mineral—we must extract the Principles or Elements essential to our Work, using the *Universal Menstruum* for retrogradation.

XVIII

This Feminine Subject cannot undergo retrogradation unless freed from her Impurities and Heterogeneous Qualities. To accomplish this, she must be actuated by her Homogeneous ones, rendering her more capable of receiving the spiritual Love of our *Green Dragon*.

XIX

Once our *Serpent* has been bound with her Chain, infused with the Blood of our *Green Dragon*, and driven nine or ten times through combustible Fire into the elementary Air, she must become exceedingly furious and highly penetrating. If she does not, it indicates that you have missed the correct Subject or misunderstood the notion of the *Homogenea* or their Proportion.

XX

If, after nine or ten cycles of Dissolution by the *Universal Menstruum*, followed by filtration, evaporation, and congealment, this furious *Serpent* does not ascend in a Cloud and transform into our *Virgin Milk* —or *Metallic Argentin Water*—which is non-corrosive yet insensibly and invisibly devours all that comes near it, then it becomes evident that you have misunderstood the true Notion of our *Universal Menstruum*.

XXI

I now refer to the *Serpent*, our actual *Water of the Clouds*—the genuine *Eagle* and *Mercury of the Philosophers*. Unlike the Vulgar *Mercury*, which is corporeal, gross, lifeless, and full of Heterogeneous Qualities— having fallen from its Sphere like unripe Fruit from the Tree—ours is spiritual, transparent, and living, residing in its Sphere like a King upon his Throne.

XXII

Although the Vulgar *Mercury* is an unripe, corporeal, and lifeless Fruit, if you know how to amalgamate it with our *Dragon* and to retrograde it using the *Universal Menstruum*, you may confidently prepare a *Sophic Mercury*. With it, you will undoubtedly produce the *Great Elixir*, discover the *Secret of Secrets*, unlock the most impenetrable Locks, and command all the Treasures of the World.

XXIII

We call our *Mercury* the *Mercury of the Philosophers* because it is not readily available to our hand; it must be prepared through our Philosophical Processes from the original *Chaos*. Although the preparation is Artificial, it is natural in its method, as Nature itself contributes by being faithfully imitated throughout the process.

XXIV

Our Subject cannot be called the fiery *Serpent of the Philosophers*, nor can it possess the power to overcome any created thing until it receives the Virtue and Quality of our *Green Dragon* and the *Universal Menstruum*. These forces must first overcome, devour, and bury it in their Bowels. Once reborn from them, the Subject acquires the same power—demonstrating that the ability to kill and vivify is intrinsic to both our *Dragon* and the *Universal Menstruum*.

XXV

The *Universal Menstruum* of the Philosophers is that Celestial substance without which nothing can exist. It is also the noble Champion who delivers the uncorrupted Virgin *Andromeda*, chained to the Rock and held under the power of the *Dragon*. Upon accepting his spiritual love—lest she be eternally devoured—she is rescued by the Champion and gives birth to a Child, who becomes the *Wonder of Wonders* and a *Prodigy of Nature*.

XXVI

If, during her Confinement, our *Virgin* does not exhibit her extreme Beauty—manifested through diverse, delicate natural Colors that are wonderfully charming and pleasing to the Eye—prior to her liberation, it signifies that she has not sufficiently partaken of the spiritual Company of the *Dragon*.

XXVII

Suppose the *Universal Menstruum* does not entirely deliver the *Virgin* from the Claws of the *Dragon*. In that case, it indicates either that she was not sufficiently purged of her Heterogeneous Qualities, lacked the necessary penetrating Quality induced by external Heat, or that the *Universal Menstruum* proved too weak to complete its Undertaking.

XXVIII

To know whether the Amalgamation, Sublimation, Dissolution, Filtration, Coagulation, and Distillation have been Natural and Philosophical, the entire Body of the *Serpent* must emerge spiritual and transparent, leaving behind only a few light Feces at the bottom—material that no Art can reduce into running *Mercury* or any other metallic Substance.

XXIX

After completing the aforementioned Operations and Separation, if our *Serpent*, when amalgamated with any Metal—pure or impure—cannot endure Fusion, it will be futile to proceed further. You may then be assured that you are not following the true Paths of the *Hermetic Art*.

XXX

Our Philosophical Distillations consist solely in the precise separation of our Spiritual and *Mercurial Water* from its poisonous oily Substance, which serves no purpose in our Art, and from the *Caput Mortuum*, the inert residue left behind after the first Distillation.

XXXI

If, after the first Distillation, an exceedingly corrosive and highly penetrating red Oil does not ascend—which, as soon as it appears in the Neck of the Retort, the Receiver must be changed—it indicates that the Distillation was not correctly performed. Consequently, the internal Fire of our metallic vaporous *Water*, consumed and corroded by its poisonous Vapor and the external Fire, remains intermixed with the *Caput Mortuum* and the impure residue.

XXXII

Should you commit a grave Error during the first Distillation, preparing the *Mercury duplex* of the Philosophers without restarting the entire Work from the beginning will become impossible. Nevertheless, if you possess further skill in our Art, you may still successfully prepare our *Mercury simplex*, allowing you to accomplish outstanding and miraculous achievements.

XXXIII

Through its mere Fumes, this blood-red Oil penetrates every Part and Atom of all Metals and Minerals, especially Gold. One can easily extract the correct Tincture or Essence from this Dissolution using a highly rectified *Spirit of Wine*, subsequently distilling it through the Alembic. This extraction yields a potent Medicine that is highly beneficial to human Bodies.

XXXIV

A deep blood-red Tincture of excellent Virtue can also be extracted from the *Caput Mortuum*, which has been accidentally and unfortunately intermixed with the internal Sulphur of our *Mercurial Water* and the red Oil. Using highly rectified *Spirit of Wine*, and after evaporation to a Powder, Imbibition, and Philosophical Digestion, you may confidently obtain the *Medicine of Medicines*—second only to the *Great Elixir*—capable of quickly and imperceptibly curing all manner of Distempers, to the great Admiration of all *Galenists* and the Astonishment of all Vulgar Chemists.

XXXV

Most Philosophers, while they Intended to go further to the noblest Perfection of our *Celestial Art*, employed this red Oil—once rendered potable—either as internal Medicine or for the treatment of external Diseases, without further preparation, until they had obtained the *Great Elixir*.

XXXVI

Suppose the *Caput Mortuum* lacks the Magnetic Quality to attract the *Spiritus Mundi* into itself from the *Astrums*. In that case, it signifies that, by the end of the Distillation of the red Oil, the external Fire was so violent as to completely burn up the Magnet contained within the first Feces of our *Mercurial Water*.

XXXVII

After the first Distillation, if even the slightest portion of the Virgin *Mercurial Water* can, by any means, be converted into running *Mercury* or any other Metallic Substance, it provides clear evidence that either the Subject or its Preparation and Reduction into Water was neither real, natural, nor Philosophical.

XXXVIII

Although the *Spiritus Mundi* plays no role in our Great Work, it nevertheless serves as a powerful *Menstruum* for extracting Tinctures from Metals, Minerals, Animals, and Vegetables and for performing remarkable feats in the Art, especially in volatilizing all fixed Bodies and principally Gold.

XXXIX

Many Pretenders to True *Hermetic Knowledge* prepare *Menstruums* designed to dissolve common *Mercury* and convert it into Water through various methods, including adding Salts, Sulphurs, Metals, and

Minerals. However, because all such preparations are sophisticated, anyone well-versed in our Art can easily reduce it back to its running Quality.

XL

The Quality of our *Mercurial Water* is to volatilize all fixed Bodies and fix all volatile ones. It fixes itself to the fixed Bodies according to its Proportion, dissolving its own Body and uniting inseparably with it, always preserving its inherent Qualities and Properties, and receiving no Augmentation from any other created thing except its own crude Body.

XLI

Our *Mercurial Water* possesses such profound sympathy with the *Astrums* that, if it is not kept tightly closed and *Hermetically* sealed, it will soon, like a winged *Serpent*, ascend marvelously to its own Sphere, carrying with it all the Elements and Principles of Metals, and leaving behind neither a single drop nor the slightest residue.

XLII

Several Pretenders to *Magical Science* prepare so-called Magical Magnets to draw *Menstruums* from the Air and, allegedly, from the *Astrums*, believing them necessary for producing the *Great Elixir*. However, because these Magnets are compounded from multiple determined substances, even though their *Menstruums* serve as potent Dissolvents, we affirm with certainty that they can never accomplish any real Experiment in our Art.

XLIII

Some claim that unless the Operator is a Master of *Magical Science* and thoroughly understands its Experiments, they can never produce the Universal *Elixir* by any other Art. Although we do not deny that Magical Knowledge enhances the attainment of Perfection across the Sciences, we are entirely sure that such knowledge is not necessary for forming the *Grand Elixir* of Animals, Metals, Precious Stones, or Vegetables.

XLIV

Our *Virgin Milk*, or *Metallic Water*, is called the true *Chaos of the Philosophers* when brought to perfect Spirituality and excellent Diaphaneity. From this alone—without the addition of any created or artificially prepared substance—we prepare and separate all the Elements necessary for Forming our *Philosophical Microcosm*.

XLV

To properly understand how to form our *Philosophical Microcosm* out of this *Chaos*, we must first comprehend the great Mystery and Method employed in the Creation of the *Macrocosm*. It is essential to imitate and apply the same method that the Creator of all things used in forming the great Universe when creating our own lesser one.

XLVI

When our *Chaos* or *Celestial Water* purifies itself from its gross and palpable Body, it is called the *Heaven of the Philosophers*. In contrast, the palpable Body is called the *Earth*, characterized by void, emptiness, and darkness. If our *Divine Spirit*, carried upon the Face of the Waters, did not extract the precious Metallic Seed from the palpable Body, we would be unable, by any Art whatsoever, to continue the perfect Creation of our *Microcosm* according to our Intent.

XLVII

After separating itself from the *Earth*, along with the Philosophical Seed, the Magnet of our *Salt of Nature*, and the superfluous Waters, the *Heaven of the Philosophers* is known as the *Mercury simplex* of the wise. Whoever attains it simultaneously gains the Knowledge and Power to retrogradate Metals, Minerals, and more—reducing them to their first Being, perfecting imperfect Bodies, vivifying dead ones, while conserving its Property and Quality—and thus can produce the *Great Elixir* according to the customary practices of the Philosophers.

XLVIII

Once we have separated the Water from the Waters—specifically the *Mercurial Celestial Water* from the superfluous Water, known as the *Phlegm*—by the blessing of God and the Infusion of our holy Spirit, we are fully confident that we shall bring forth from our *Earth* such Fruits and Subjects as will enable us to perform the complete Creation, carrying our Work to the highest Degree of Perfection.

XLIX

Given that our *Mercurial Water* shares the same brightness as the Heavens, and our palpable, gross Body—having separated itself from the *Celestial Water*—possesses the same Properties and Quality as the *Earth*, only Ignorance would deny that they constitute the True *Heaven* and *Earth* of the Philosophers.

L

If, after the Separation of the Spirit from the superfluous Waters, the resulting World does not appear exceedingly clear, full of light, and possessing the same brightness as our *Celestial Water*, it signifies that the Separation was incomplete and that the Spirit remains intermixed with the Waters.

LI

If, within nine or ten Weeks—or two Philosophical Months at the latest—our *Mercurial Water* has not fully separated itself from its own *Earth*, containing the Metallic Seed, it indicates that you have either erred in its working or that the Digestion was too violent, thereby confounding and burning up the principal Subject of the Creation.

LII

This *Philosophic Earth*, containing our principal Subject, must be gently dried by external Heat after being separated from all Waters to free it from extraneous Humidity. This method prepares it to properly receive the Celestial Moisture of our *Argentin Water*, which unites its most noble Fruits—nourishing, generating, and saturating our *Philosophical Microcosm*.

LIII

If, after reverberation and humectation with our *Celestial Moisture*, the *Earth* does not immediately enrich the Air with the expected divine Fruits, it must be concluded that the external Heat during drying was so violent as to burn up the internal Heat and Nature of the *Earth*, thereby spoiling your Undertaking and preventing the full performance of the Mystery of the Creation according to the noblest, richest, shortest, most natural, and most secret ways of the Philosophers.

LIV

If the *Earth* is destroyed by violent external Heat, continuing our noble Creation with it becomes impossible. Nevertheless, if you know how to amalgamate our *Mercury simplex* with common Gold—dissolved, vivified, and renewed by it—you may still succeed in effecting the *Great Elixir*. However, not as quickly, naturally, or richly as you would have without such destruction. This constitutes our third method.

LV

The Amalgamation of our *Mercury simplex* with standard Gold depends solely on achieving the correct Proportion and an indissoluble Union of both substances. This Union occurs without applying external Heat and in a very short time. Without exact Proportion and proper Union, nothing of significance can be expected from their Marriage.

LVI

Understand that the correct Proportion is ten parts of our *Mercury simplex* to one part of your finest standard Gold in filings, which dissolves within it imperceptibly, like ice in common Water. As soon as the Dissolution is complete, Coagulation and Putrefaction immediately follow. If these effects do not manifest, it signifies that the *Mercury* exceeds its proper Proportion. Once your Gold has been well amalgamated, united, putrefied, and inseparably digested with our *Mercury simplex*, you will possess only our *Philosophical Sulphur*. The entire Work could have been performed at that stage without using common Gold.

LVII

Although our *Mercury simplex* is exceedingly spiritual and volatile because it is the correct Agent for digesting the Seed or Essence of all Metals and Minerals, it will, even while undigested, naturally adhere to any corporeal Metal or Mineral it encounters. It will not separate from the Metal unless forcibly removed by the Test, even when kept in excellent Fusion for many hours.

LVIII

This *Mercury simplex* exhibited a Feminine Nature prior to its retrogradation. Before it separated from its own *Earth*, it was *Hermaphroditic*, powerful in both Sexes. It has now reverted to a Feminine Quality. Although it has lost its visible Masculine Fire, it retains its internal Fire, invisible to us, through which it performs visible Operations in digesting imperfect Metals once Determined with any of them.

LIX

Suppose our *Mercury*, with the correct Proportion observed, is amalgamated with any imperfect Metal after being first determined with a fixed one. In that case, it will regenerate and perfect that Metal without losing the slightest Particle of its Virtue or Quantity. After the Digestion of a Philosophical Month, the regenerated Metal will, as most

Philosophers teach, withstand all Trials and surpass any Naturally occurring Metal in excellence.

LX

The Determination of our *Mercury simplex* with any fixed Body is accomplished by dissolving a small number of Filings—either red or white—according to the Color and Quality of the Metal you seek to improve. If you commit no error in the Separation and Union of the Subjects, you may confidently expect to achieve your desired result after a Philosophical Digestion.

LXI

To properly examine whether the *Mercury simplex* is rightly prepared or has reached Perfection, place a single Drop upon a red-hot Plate of Copper. The Drop must whiten the Copper completely and remain attached even under excellent Fusion. If it fails, it Demonstrates that the *Mercury* is unprepared or has not entirely separated from its own *Earth*.

LXII

If your *Mercury simplex,* put upon its own dried *Earth*, does not presently unite with the Essence of Metals, appearing deeper than any Blood and shining brighter than any Fire, which is a mark of the Reception of its internal Fire, and that the Eagle has sucked the Blood of our *Red-Lion*, it is an evident sign, that you have errored in the Manipulation of the *Earth*.

LXIII

This *Mercury*, impregnated with its Essence or the Sulphur of Metals, is called the *Mercury duplex of the Philosophers*, possessing far greater Quality and Virtue than the *simplex*. Through its Imbibitions in the *Salt of Nature*, after saturation with the *simplex*, the entire Mystery of the Creation of the *Philosophical Microcosm* is maintained and perfected.

LXIV

To determine whether your *Mercury duplex* is Philosophically prepared and sufficiently impregnated with its internal Natural Fire, place a single Drop upon a red-hot Plate of fine Silver. Suppose the Drop does not penetrate the Silver with a deep-red Tincture capable of enduring the most significant Fire of Fusion. In that case, it signifies that you have either failed in its Preparation or have not allowed sufficient time for it to receive full Saturation from its own *Earth*.

LXV

This deep-red Tincture, extracted from our *Philosophical Earth*, is called our *Sulphur*, our undigested *essentiated Gold*, our internal *elementary Fire*, and our *Red-Lion*. Without its Help and Concurrence, our *Philosophical World* cannot be nourished, digested, or completed, as it constitutes the proper Ground and essential Essence of the entire Work of our Creation.

LXVI

When the *Earth* has lost its Soul, the remainder becomes the true Magnet, attracting the *Salt of Nature* from the combustible Fire after undergoing violent Calcination for several hours. This *Salt*, after its Purification and Clarification, is called the *clarified Earth* or the *Salt of the Philosophers*. Upon uniting with our single and double *Mercury* after their Digestion, it is referred to by our Master *Hermes* as the *Universal Spirit earthified*.

LXVII

Our *Mercury simplex* must perform the Extraction, Purification, and Clarification of our *Earth* or *Salt of Nature*. When placed upon the reverberated *Earth*, it will immediately draw the *Earth* to itself and unite with it, yet it remains separable through gentle Distillation. After this process, the *clarified Salt of the Philosophers* is obtained.

LXVIII

Although we employ our *Mercury simplex* in the Extraction of its Soul from its Body and the Clarification of the latter, it remains a Philosophical and perpetual *Menstruum*. It loses nothing of its connatural Prerogatives and does not diminish in Quantity, being our true *Alkahest*, as *Paracelsus* names it.

LXIX

The three Principles, or Elements, of our *Chaos*, once perfectly separated from their Impurities and brought to their highest Perfection, are called the *three Herculean Works*. After preparing these, all Labor, Trouble, and Danger will be overcome.

LXX

Some foolish Operators claim that our *Great Elixir* can be prepared easily and without trouble. To them, we, along with our Master *Hermes*, briefly reply: such Imposters neither know our *Matter* nor the correct Preparation of it. Yet we do not deny that any Healthy Person, regardless of age, may successfully undertake all our *Herculean* Labors necessary for its Performance.

LXXI

We call these Operations *Herculean* in contrast to the remainder of the Work, which is exceedingly easy and without the least Trouble or Danger. For this reason, it is termed *Children's Play*, as even a Child or a Woman with basic understanding may efficiently conduct it and bring it to the highest Perfection, according to the teaching of all true Philosophers.

LXXII

Although the Philosophers commonly regard the above-mentioned Operations as complex and dangerous, we can, upon our Conscience, assure you that we have personally prepared them all without assistance from any living being, using only a common Kitchen Fire. This fact is well known to several *Coadepts*, our Friends, who could not help but admire and approve of our Industry.

LXXIII

No true *Adept* or perfect *Artist* can deny that the entire Work of the *Great Elixir* may be performed from beginning to end using only one Furnace, one type of Vessel, and a single Person, all at a very small Charge.

LXXIV

Some imposters attempt to persuade the Vulgar that Gold, Silver, and many other Ingredients are necessary to create the *Grand Elixir* according to our noblest methods. However, the Doctrines of all the Philosophers and our own infallible Rules demonstrate this as false. It is most certain that we will not use any of these Ingredients, nor will we use any Silver or Gold (except, as previously mentioned, in our third way) until we reach the Fermentation of our *Elixirs*.

LXXV

Together with all true Philosophers, we assure you that everything necessary for our *Philosophical Work*—apart from the Fuel, Vessels, and a few Instruments belonging to the Furnace—can be purchased for less than the cost of a single Guinea and that such items are obtainable everywhere and at all times of the year.

LXXVI

Since neither Gold nor Silver is used in the Formation or Cibation of our *Philosophical Work*, it follows that the old and common saying of some Authors—namely, *that without working with Gold, it is impossible to make Gold*—proves to be merely a false Notion held by those who do not understand our Art.

LXXVII

When our *Herculean* Works are brought to Perfection—when our three Principles or Elements are prepared, purified, and perfected—the *Great Mystery of our Creation* cannot be expected unless the Philosophical and inseparable Union of them is performed with exactness.

LXXVIII

When our Principles or Elements are brought to a perfect and inseparable Union and Digestion, they are called the *Triple Mercury of the Philosophers*. The entire Creation and Formation of our Work is crowned upon its completion.

LXXIX

All our Work of the Creation, from its very Beginning to its perfect End, may, to our specific knowledge, be completed in less than nine Months by any skillful and careful Artist who follows our Rules, unless some Accident occurs during the Preparation of our *Herculean* Works. To prevent such mishaps, we performed the Work ourselves in an earthen Vessel, which we consider far better and surer than any Glass and most agreeable to the Practice of the most ancient Philosophers.

LXXX

Before proceeding to the Union of your Elements, you must first digest your clarified *Earth* in a moderate and continual Heat of Ashes to free it from any unnatural Moisture it may have attracted after its Purification. This ensures it is in a proper Capacity to receive your *Mercury simplex*, by which it will be nourished in its Infancy.

LXXXI

If your clarified *Earth*, after being digested for a whole Month, does not appear exceedingly dry, subtle, and frangible, it signifies that you have either failed in its Purification or Clarification or that the external Moisture it attracted has not yet been fully separated.

LXXXII

Take great Care not to begin the Imbibitions of your *Earth* until you find it thoroughly purified, clarified, dried, and rendered very subtle and extremely frangible. Beginning your Imbibitions prematurely would have significant Detrimental effects on your Work and your *Mercury*. Although it may not entirely spoil the Work, it would result in a considerable loss of time.

LXXXIII

After our clarified *Earth* has reached perfect Purity, Dryness, and Frangibility, it must be imbibed with the eighth part of our *Mercury simplex*, or *Virgin's Milk*. Our *Mercury* will be absorbed quickly, like Water, into a Sponge, indicating the hungry State of our Infant. The Fire must continue until the Infant becomes hungry again.

LXXXIV

If, within two or three days—or four at the farthest—the Infant does not display extreme hunger by becoming very dry and frangible again, it signifies that it has been overwhelmed by excessively feeding it.

LXXXV

Take great care when feeding the noble Infant. If you fail to carefully observe all our infallible Rules, you will never bring it to perfect Maturity. For in the correct Notion and Proportion of our Imbibitions, and their proper Management, the prosperous and unfailing End of our Work is to be expected.

LXXXVI

It must always be observed that the Fire remains very moderate during your Imbibitions to prevent any part of your *Mercury* from being forced to leave the *Earth*. Just as a moderate Heat creates the Union between the Soul and the Body and perfects the entire Work, a violent Heat also disunites and destroys all.

LXXXVII

Once the Infant is dry, you must repeat the Imbibition, continuing this Method until the *Matter* has received its full weight of *Mercury*. At that point, if you do not find it flowing like Wax, appearing whiter than any Snow, and exhibiting great Fixity, you must continue your Imbibitions until these qualities are fully achieved.

LXXXVIII

Imbibitions must not be performed more often than once every three or four days. During this interval, you will observe that your *Matter*, having absorbed all your *Mercury*, will greatly need Food, which must be supplied until it becomes fully saturated. The indication of this saturation is when the *Matter* again flows like Wax.

LXXXIX

Know that you have perfected the *white Elixir* when your *Matter* has been brought to perfect Fluxibility, incomparable Whiteness, and unalterable Fixedness. Fermented with fine Silver in Filings, it can transmute all inferior Metals into the finest Silver in the World.

XC

Before the *white Elixir* is fermented with common Silver, you may multiply it—both in Virtue and in Quantity—through the Continued Imbibitions with the *Mercury simplex*, by which it may gradually be brought *ad infinitum* in its Virtue.

XCI

When the *white Elixir* has reached its Degree of Maturity and seeks its highest Degree of Perfection, it must not be fermented with Silver. Instead, it must be cibated with its own Flesh and Blood, the *double Mercury*. The whole Work is accomplished through this nourishment, multiplication in Quality and Quantity, and proper Digestion.

XCII

As soon as the first Imbibition is completed, you will observe a significant Alteration within your Vessel, for a Cloud will fill the entire space, with the fixed contending against the Volatile and the Volatile against the fixed. Although the Volatile prevails at the beginning, it is ultimately, by its own internal Fire conjoined with the external, that both are united and fixed inseparably.

XCIII

It must be observed that the Glass Vessel—oval in shape, with a Neck half a foot long and very strong—must be of appropriate size and Capacity, such that your *Matter*, when placed inside, occupies only one-third of the Vessel, leaving the other two-thirds vacant. If the Vessel is too large, it will hinder the performance of the Work; if it is too small, it will break into a thousand pieces.

XCIV

After cibating the noble *Elixir* with your double *Mercury*, it must pass through all the States and Colors of Nature before reaching perfect Fixedness. Through these transformations, we can judge its Being and Temperament.

XCV

The constant and essential Colors that appear during the Digestion of the *Matter* and before it reaches Perfection are three: Black, which signifies the Putrefaction and Conjunction of the Elements; White, which demonstrates its Purification; and Red, which denotes its

Maturation. All other Colors that appear and disappear during the Progress of the Work are accidental and inconstant.

XCVI

Through each Cibation of its own Flesh and Blood, each Regeneration of its Colors, and each stage of Digestion, the Infant will grow stronger and stronger. At last, when it is fully saturated and digested, it becomes the *Great Elixir of the Philosophers*, with which you can perform Wonders across all Regions—Animal, Mineral, and Vegetable alike.

XCVII

When your *Elixir* has reached Fluxibility and perfect Fixedness, you must determine or ferment it with common Gold in Filings if you desire to create a Medicine for Metals. This Determination will vitrify, and you will obtain an incomparable Medicine capable of transmuting all imperfect Metals into the purest Gold, according to the Doctrine of all Philosophers. However, we never intended anything other than a universal Remedy for Curing all curable Diseases related to Human Bodies, as is well known to our Friends who have enjoyed the Benefits of our labor.

XCVIII

It must be observed during Fermentation that the *Elixir* does not exceed the *Ferment* in Quantity; otherwise, the Sponsal Ligament cannot be appropriately performed; conversely, if the *Ferment* predominates over the *Elixir*, the entire composition will immediately be reduced to dust.

XCIX

The best method of Fermentation is to take one part of the *Elixir* and place it amid ten parts of Gold in Filings, which have been cast through Antimony to remove all Impurities. Keep the mixture in a circulary Fire for six hours, gradually increasing the Fire to reach a good Fusion during the final two hours. When cooled, you will find your *Matter* exceedingly frangible and bearing the Color of the Garnet-Stone.

C

Common *Mercury*, amalgamated with Lead, is regarded as the most proper Subject for making Projection. Divide your fermented *Matter* into three parts once the Amalgam is in Fusion. Roll one part in Wax and immediately cast it upon the Amalgam; then promptly cover the Crucible and continue the Fire until you hear the Noise of Separation and Union. Repeat the same process with the second and third parts. Afterward, maintain a continual Fire of Fusion for two hours, then allow it to cool naturally.

CI

Whoever presumes to prepare the *Great Elixir* according to our most Secret Ways without following and observing all these infallible Rules will certainly find themselves mightily mistaken, having, after much Trouble, Expense, and Pain, reaped nothing but Discontent. Conversely, those who walk in our actual and infallible Paths shall attain their desired End with very little Trouble and Expense—a success we cordially wish to all sincere well-wishers of the *Hermetic Philosophy*.

FINIS.

Introduction

TO ALL TRUE LOVERS OF THE HERMETIC PHILOSOPHY.

H*aving in our precedent,* Aphorisms *delivered the infallible Rules and Instructions necessary for producing our Grand Elixir, or* Circulatum Majus—*the only real Secret of the true* Adepts, *which commands in all the Kingdoms of Nature—we do not doubt that this will be as pleasing to all lovers of the Sciences as it is to our Disciples. Being further inclined to fully inform them how to preserve themselves and others in perfect Health by preventing any Distemper that may otherwise overcome them before they attain the Accomplishment of their Desires, we have judged it fitting also to impart our three distinct methods for preparing our Vegetable* Elixir, *or* Circulatum Minus.

This Elixir may be prepared and brought to its utmost Perfection within the space of a Philosophical Month by any skillful Artist who comprehends and follows the specific Directions laid out in these subsequent Aphorisms. *The Work here has demonstrated that none—even those slightly versed in* Chemistry—*should be liable for mistakes.*

Nor do we doubt that all who peruse these written Aphorisms *with sincere and upright Intentions will feel compelled to bless Almighty God for His infinite Mercy in inspiring us to open their Eyes so that they may see what is necessary for their present Health and future Happiness. Both of these we heartily wish to everyone who—as becomes a true Philosopher—unfeignedly loves God and his Neighbor.*

The Vegetable Elixir
CIRCULATUM MINUS

I

Our *Circulatum Minus* is a specificated *Elixir* belonging to the
Vegetable Kingdom, by which, without any Fire or further Preparation
of the Vegetables, we can instantly extract their true Essence, containing
their Virtue, Quality, and Property. This process represents a great
Chemical Curiosity, performing Wonders in the Practice of Physics and
demonstrating certain Works of Nature.

II

We call it *Circulatum* because, no matter how often it is used in any
Extraction or *Chemical Experiment*, it loses nothing of its Quality or
Property. This is a Prerogative belonging to the Universal *Elixir*, also
called the *Circulatum Majus*, because it commands all three Kingdoms
of Nature, whereas this *Circulatum Minus*, being restricted to only one
Kingdom, is so named for that reason.

III

Out of *Diana's* undetermined Tears when *Apollo* appeared, and after the Separation of the three Elements, Determination, Digestion, and glorious Resurrection, we can prepare this determined *Elixir* without adding any other created thing. This constitutes the Philosopher's first, noblest, and most secret way.

IV

The Determination of our *Diana's Tears* consists solely in their perfect and indissoluble Union with the fixed Vegetable *Earth*, philosophically prepared, purified, and spiritualized. For the love of this *Earth*, they are compelled to abandon their first universal undetermined Property and become clothed with a determined, particular one, which is necessary to prepare our *Circulatum Minus*.

V

Our second method of preparing this *Vegetable Elixir* involves the correct Manipulation of a Plant of the noblest Degree, standing alone or supported by others. After its Preparation, Putrefaction, Reduction into an Oil, Separation of the three Principles, and their subsequent Purification, Union, and Spiritualization, the whole is transformed into a spiritual, ever-living Fountain capable of renewing every Plant immersed in it.

VI

The third and more common method is simply a Conjunction of a fixed Vegetable *Salt* with its own volatile sulphureous *Spirit*, which can be ready and prepared by any Vulgar *Chemist*. However, because the purest *Sulphur*, containing the Soul, suffers some Detriment through non-philosophical manipulation, they cannot be inseparably joined without a sulphureous *Medium*. Through this *Medium*, the Soul is strengthened, and the Body and Spirit are capable of a perfect Union.

VII

The proper *Medium* required for the indissoluble Union of these two

Subjects is a sulphureous and bituminous *Matter* issuing from a Plant, either living or dead, found in various parts of the World and known to all manner of Men (with the *Copavian* being the best, followed by the *Italian*). After separation from its feculent parts through our Universal *Menstruum*, all the Pores and Atoms of the fixed Vegetable *Salt*—greatly fortified by it—are dilated, making it capable of receiving its own *Spirit* and uniting inseparably with it.

VIII

To fortify the *Sulphur* and open the Pores of the *Salt*, imbibe the *Salt* with the bituminous *Matter* using moderate digestive Heat as if one were hatching Chickens. The Imbibitions must be repeated as the Salt dries until it becomes fully saturated and refuses to absorb more of the *Matter*.

IX

During Imbibitions, the entire Mass must be stirred at least nine or ten times a day with a *Spatula* or another Instrument made of dry Wood. Through this reiterated Motion, the bituminous *Matter* gains better ingress into the Body and more quickly perfects its Operation.

X

Great Care must be taken during the performance of the Imbibitions to prevent any Soil or Dust from falling into your *Matter*. To prevent contamination, keep the Vessel covered with Paper pricked full of holes or another suitable Covering. Additionally, nothing containing its own internal *Sulphur* should come near the Vessel, for the Pores of the *Salt*, being highly dilated and opened, may easily determine themselves toward another Subject and thereby spoil your Undertaking.

XI

If, within three or four Weeks at the farthest, your fixed Vegetable *Salt* does not manifest full Saturation, it will be in vain for you to proceed any further with it. You may be assured that you have either erred in the Notion of the *Salt*, identifying the authentic sulphureous *Medium*, or Managing the Imbibitions.

XII

When your Imbibitions are fully completed, your *Salt* will then be appropriately prepared to receive its own *Spirit*, by which it becomes volatile, spiritual, transparent, and wonderfully penetrating, entering immediately into the Pores and Particles of every Vegetable and instantly separating their true Essence or Elements.

XIII

Although the *Salt* is fully prepared for the Reception of its own *Spirit*, unless you carefully observe the correct Proportion between them— namely, that the volatile must always predominate over the fixed—you will never achieve a perfect Union between these two Subjects, which are contrary in Quality, though not in Nature.

XIV

A Putrefaction of eight to ten days must precede before beginning your Distillations and Cohobations, following the Addition of the Vegetable *Spirit* to its own *Salt*. During this time, the sulphureous *Spirit*, strengthened by the bituminous *Matter* and finding the *Salt* fit for Conjunction, gains the power to enter into its Pores, thereby facilitating its Volatilization and Union.

XV

If, after six or seven Distillations and Cohobations of the distilled liquid upon the Remainder, you do not find your *Spirit* to be extremely sharp and the remainder at the bottom altogether insipid, it will be clear that you lack proper knowledge of the Vegetable *Spirit*. Being exceedingly volatile by Nature, it possesses the power to volatilize its own Body and inseparably unite with it, provided the Body is capable of its Reception.

XVI

It must be observed that during the Progress of your Distillations, the sulphureous *Medium* must not ascend in the least. Although it is a true *Medium* that concurs in uniting the Body with the *Spirit* before the Spiritualization of the Body—and without which no perfect Union of these two Subjects can be expected—its continued Concurrence during the Progress of the Work would be highly disadvantageous to both and would subvert your Operation.

XVII

The ascent of the sulphureous *Medium* when the *Spirit* begins to carry over its own Body to unite inseparably with it clearly and certainly signifies that you are not regulating your Fire properly. Instead of applying a gentle vaporous Heat to facilitate the Union, you use a violent Heat that destroys it.

XVIII

When your *Salt* is brought to perfect Spiritualization and genuine Union with its own volatile *Spirit*, you will then have in your possession your *Circulatum Minus*, or *Vegetable Elixir* and *Menstruum*, with which you will be able to perform wonders within the Vegetable Kingdom—separating in a moment not only their Principles or Elements but also, in the same Operation, the Pure from the Impure.

XIX

If you place any green Vegetable, shredded into pieces, into your *Vegetable Elixir*, it will, in less than half a quarter of an hour and without any external Heat, putrefy and precipitate itself to the bottom, quite dead (being nothing but the cursed Excremental *Earth*). A yellow Oil containing the *Salt* and *Sulphur* will float on top, and the *Elixir* will take on the Color of the Plant, encompassing its Vegetable *Spirit*. It is a clear sign that your Operations have not been Philosophical if it does not.

XX

A single drop of this yellowish Oil, administered in cases of Distemper according to the Virtue and Quality attributed to the Plant, given every Morning and Evening in a Glass of Wine or another convenient Vehicle, will infallibly and insensibly cure such Distempers. It will also corroborate the vital Spirits if taken consistently to purify the Blood during sickly and infectious Times.

XXI

If you place Coral into this *Menstruum*, you will witness an admirable Experiment. Although its Pores are more compact than those of any other Vegetable, it will suddenly transmit its internal *Spirit* into the *Menstruum*, sending its Soul and Body, like a blood-red Oil, to the surface and eventually precipitating as a grayish Excrement at the Bottom.

XXII

If Myrrh, Aloes, and Saffron, in equal Quantities, are placed into this *Menstruum*, the truest *Elixir Proprietatis* (as *Paracelsus* terms it)—a most excellent Cordial and almost as Efficacious and Virtuous as the Universal *Elixir* itself in curing all curable Distempers—will immediately rise to the surface. At the same time, its *Caput Mortuum* will separate and settle at the Bottom.

XXIII

This *Vegetable Menstruum* dissolves not only all sorts of Gums and other kinds of Substances within the Vegetable Kingdom but also all varieties of Oils and Balsams extracted from Trees, separating their true Essence. Through this Essence, you may perform wonderful operations upon both living and dead Bodies, preserved indefinitely without opening or any further Preparation.

XXIV

Although this *Menstruum* is specificated only for Vegetables, it will nevertheless, in a moment, draw the Tincture out of Metals and Minerals. However, it will not separate all their Principles, as it is not the appropriate *Menstruum* for such Operations. Although such Sulphurs are highly balsamic for the Lungs and Spleen, since our *Elixir Proprietatis* far surpasses these preternatural Preparations, we present this merely as a curious Chemical Experiment.

XXV

Since this *Vegetable Menstruum* is eternal, you must ensure that you lose nothing of its Quantity or Quality when separating it from the Oil and Spirit of the Vegetable. This separation is accomplished by a gentle Distillation in *Balneo vaporoso*, with the Vessel well-luted and thoroughly dried beforehand. The *Menstruum* comes over with the Phlegm of the Vegetable and must be separated from it by a Distillation in *Balneo* for further use. The Oil remains at the Bottom, united with its own *Spirit*, and will easily distill over in any common Heat, leaving nothing behind. This is the Mark of its Spiritualization, Purification, and Regeneration, which it has received from the *Menstruum*.

XXVI

Out of this Oil or Essence of your Vegetable, thus prepared—or by any other Philosophical method, as we have described in our second Manner of making this *Elixir*—if you know how to putrefy it naturally without any Fire and to separate all our Principles from it, purifying and uniting them inseparably together, all rendered spiritual and transparent, you will then, through this second Regeneration, obtain the greatest *Arcanum* in the World—effective not only upon Vegetables but also upon Minerals and Metals, except Gold and Silver.

XXVII

Suppose our *first Matter* determines this regenerated Essence. In that case, it will then possess the Capacity to radically dissolve all sorts of Metals or Minerals, particularly Gold, which is imperceptibly dissolved within it, like ice in common Water. It can never again be separated as common Gold—neither by Distillation nor Digestion. From this, after a Philosophical Digestion, Separation of the three Principles, their Purification, Union, further Digestion, and third Regeneration, you may prepare the great Medicine of Medicines, possessing equal Virtue and Quality with the Grand *Elixir* upon Human Bodies, and with our *Mercury simplex* upon Metals or Minerals.

XXVIII

The Determination of this regenerated *Menstruum* with our *first Matter* is accomplished through its Amalgamation. In this process, the *Vegetable Menstruum*, drawing out all the Qualities and Properties of the *first Matter* and uniting them with its own, becomes capable of possessing the same Virtue and Property as our *Mercury simplex* in dissolving and volatilizing every created thing that comes near it.

XXIX

Some are of the Opinion that both *Elixirs* may be produced from various determined things, such as Human Excrements or *May Dew* (which they also call their *Menstruum from above* or *Water from the Clouds*), and that the Grand *Elixir* may be prepared from this or any other regenerated Vegetable *Menstruum*. However, since we know that such *Menstruums*, which they call their *Philosophical Mercury*, although capable of dissolving and volatilizing Metals, cannot meliorate any of them—this Dissolution and Volatilization being neither natural nor Philosophical—we, with good Reason, judge all these Opinions to be nothing more than false Suppositions and ill-grounded, imaginary Notions.

XXX

With our Divine Master *Hermes*, we affirm that, after Almighty God created all things and commanded each to procreate according to its own kind, our *Elixirs* are not to be produced by any of the sophistical methods. As we have fully demonstrated in these and our preceding

Aphorisms, we have provided ample Instructions for preparing the Universal *Elixir* from our undetermined *Matter* and the specificated *Elixir* from the Root of Vegetables.

XXXI

Out of true Affection and Charity for all Lovers of the Arts, we advise everyone who desires to prepare either of these *Elixirs* to follow only our Infallible Rules, which are the *Compendium* of the entire Practice and Theory according to all true Philosophers and to disregard all others. Some have delivered teachings by Hearsay, others from mere Reading, and very few from their own Practice, making it easy for them to be imposed upon and deluded by any *Pseudo-chemist* or pretended Adept.

Experto Crede.

Postscript

CONTAINING AN EXPLANATION OF THE FIGURE, PREFIXED TO THE APHORISMI URBIGERANI.

H aving in our One Hundred and One *Aphorisms* so clearly laid open all the Difficulties and so thoroughly taught the complete Theory and Practice of the whole *Hermetic Mystery*, any sincere and ingenious Lover of *Chemistry* will not only be equipped to understand the most abstruse writings of the Philosophers but also capable of executing any real Experiment expected in the Progress of our Celestial Art. However, believing that those who are not our Disciples may still encounter specific Philosophical Figures—the meanings of which may not be easily understood—we have judged it highly expedient to place our Figure at the Front of this little Book.

This Figure is a perfect *Compendium* of all the Philosophical Emblems through which the others may be easily understood. Now, because this Figure—mystically representing all our Subjects and Operations—naturally admits many and various Interpretations, it would render our *Aphorisms* (wherein these meanings are already delivered) redundant if we attempted to list them all here. For this reason, we at first judged it superfluous to offer any further Illustration.

However, in our desire to do all the good we can for the Public, upon second Thought, we have resolved—with our customary Brevity —to offer the following Explanation to aid the better Comprehension of the Figure and our *Aphorisms*.

The *Tree* serves as the Supporter of the Motto *Virtus unita fortior*. This phrase, which is to be read from the side of the *Serpent*—marked by the Half-Moon on its Head and signifying the Planet under whose Influence it is born—is to be referred back to the *Serpent* itself through its particular Motto. This indicates that, if taken alone, the *Serpent* can do little or nothing in our Art, lacking the necessary Assistance of others.

The *Green Dragon* represents our first undetermined *Matter*, which comprehends all our Principles (as signified by the Half-Moon on its Head, the Sun in its Body, and the Cross on its Tail). Its Motto affirms that it can perform the whole Work without admixture of other created or artificially prepared things: this is our first way. However, this *Dragon*, when copulating with the *Serpent*, condescends and degrades itself from its undetermined Being to give rise to our second way.

Apollo, bearing the Sun on his Head, and *Diana*, crowned with the Half-Moon, are shown embracing one another. Together, they signify our third way and the Continuation of the first and second. The *River* into which they descend represents the State into which they must be reduced before being born again—and before, in any of our three ways, they can be brought to perfect Spiritualization and Union.

Apollo and *Diana*, rising from the *River* in one glorious Body— with *Diana* having now obtained all—represent our *Herculean Works* fully completed and the beginning of their Conjunction. As they move to place their feet upon solid ground, where she is to sow the noble Fruits for future Procreation, this act symbolizes the continuation of their Conjunction until they are fully united and perfected.

Like our *Aphorisms*, this Figure also mystically exhibits the principal Points of Faith and Religion found in the Volumes of the Old and New Testament. From this, it becomes manifestly clear that the Contemplation of Nature truly leads to the Comprehension of those heavenly Verities by which alone we may hope to attain the blessed Immortality that is the true and ultimate End of our Creation—and toward which all our Endeavors must be directed.

FINIS